MW00366498

Mother's Day

by Fay Robinson
illustrated by Linda Davick

Scott Foresman

Editorial Offices: Glenview, Illinois • New York, New York
Sales Offices: Reading, Massachusetts • Duluth, Georgia
Glenview, Illinois • Carrollton, Texas • Menlo Park, California

It was Mother's Day.

Kitty made orange juice.
She was happy.

4

Kitty made a bowl of cereal.
She was singing.

Kitty made toast.
She was happy.

8

Mom will love this!

Kitty made a cup of tea.
She was pleased.

11

Kitty made a pancake.
She was pleased.

Mom will love this!

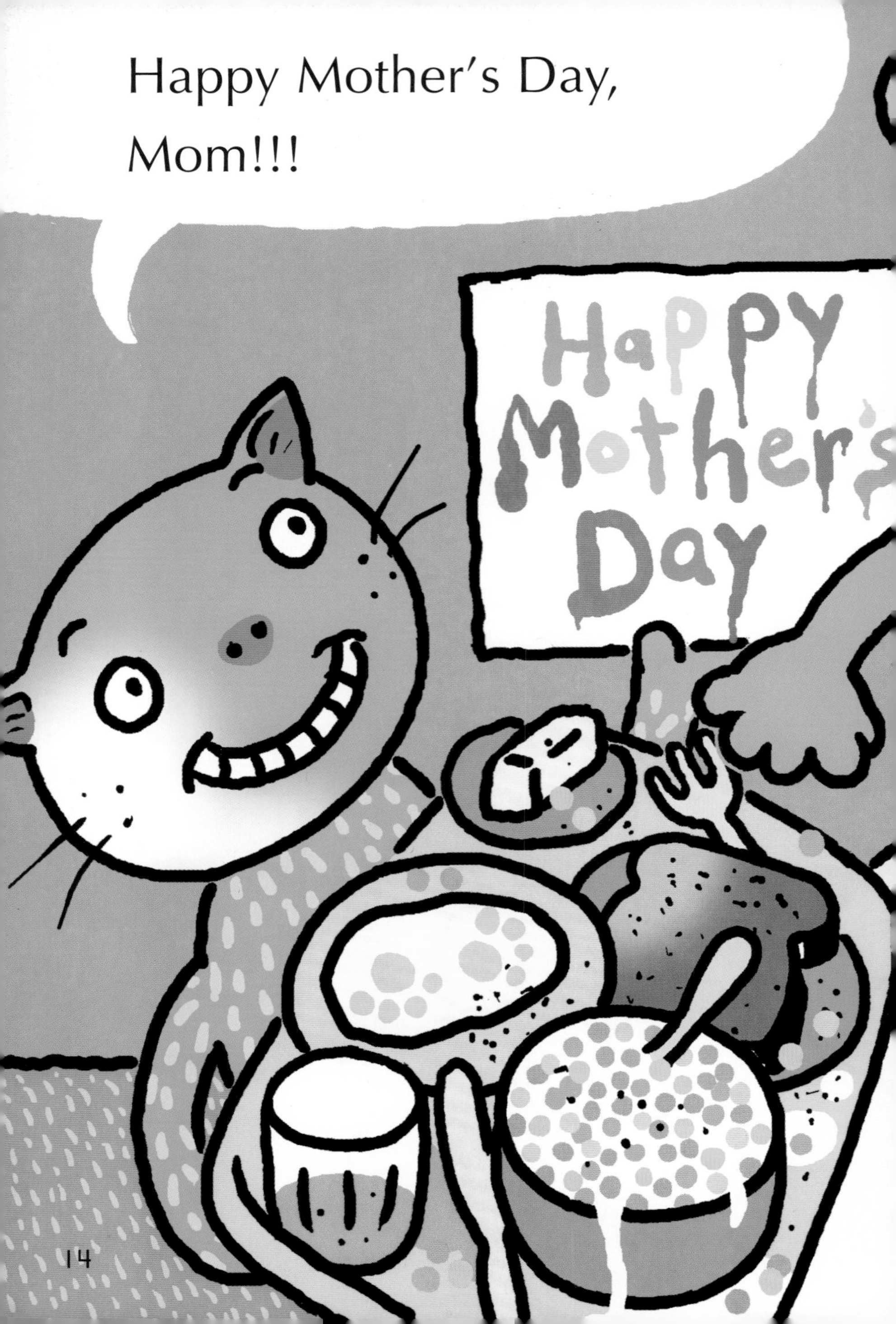
Happy Mother's Day,
Mom!!!
Happy Mother's Day

Mom was happy.
Mom was pleased.
Mom ate every bit!

16